THE MERCURY FOUNTAIN

For Chella,
with all good wishes
Gregory Warren Wilson
2013

BY THE SAME AUTHOR
Poetry
PRESERVING LEMONS
HANGING WINDCHIMES IN A VACUUM
JEOPARDY

Illustration
Antony Hopkins, MUSICAMUSINGS

Gregory Warren Wilson

THE MERCURY FOUNTAIN

ENITHARMON PRESS

First published in 2008
by Enitharmon Press
26B Caversham Road
London NW5 2DU

www.enitharmon.co.uk

Distributed in the UK by
Central Books
99 Wallis Road
London E9 5LN

Distributed in the USA and Canada
by Dufour Editions Inc.
PO Box 7, Chester Springs
PA 19425, USA

© Gregory Warren Wilson 2008

ISBN: 978-1-904634-63-8

Enitharmon Press gratefully acknowledges the
financial support of Arts Council England, London.

British Library Cataloguing-in-Publication Data.
A catalogue record for this book is available
from the British Library.

for the snow leopard, seen
or unseen, changes everything –
our attentiveness and its spots

Typeset in Albertina by Libanus Press
and printed in England by
CPI Antony Rowe

ACKNOWLEDGEMENTS

Acknowledgements are due to the editors of the following publications in which some of these poems, or earlier versions of them, first appeared: *Ambit, Anon, Chimera, Highways* (The Housman Society, 2002), *To Hell with Journals* (ed. Hisham Matar, 2007), *Magma, Modern Poetry in Translation, New Welsh Review, Poetry Greece, Poetry Review, Smiths Knoll, Soundings, Staple, The French Literary Review, The Frogmore Papers, The Interpreter's House, The London Magazine, The Rialto, The Shop, The Stinging Fly, The Wolf, Thumbscrew*. Several poems in this collection were first published under a pseudonym.

Justin Pearson and the Locrian Ensemble commissioned 'A Year in the Nail Salon' to be performed with Vivaldi's *Four Seasons*. The first performance was at the Maddermarket Theatre in Norwich with Rita Manning as soloist.

I would like to express my gratitude to Arts Council England for a grant which gave me time to work on this book. I am also grateful to Charles Beckett for his timely encouragement.

I particularly want to thank Carole Satyamurti, whose generous and insightful criticism has been invaluable over the years, and my editor, Stephen Stuart-Smith, for his inestimable help.

CONTENTS

I
THE EDGE OF POSSIBILITY

Ask Icarus	13
Transition	14
The Capsule Test	15
Vegetable Carving in the Neptune Lounge	16
Travelling with My Theremin	18
Dislocation	19
Delirium	20
Cold-blooded Sex	21
The Palace of Lassitude	22
Patterson's Curse, Salvation Jane	24
The Midnight Scholar	25
Thinking About Plantains in the Rain	26
Six Misapprehensions	27
Telling Tales	32

II
VALVES OF SENSATION

Abruptly Without Reserve	37
The Implacable Detail of Morning	38
Sleepless at Dawn	39
Admission at Almond Time	40
Metempsychosis and the Painted Lady	41
The Mercury Fountain	42

III
ALMOST LIKE A STRANGER

The Opacity of Strangeness	47
Giveaway	48
Five Kopecks to Spend After Busking	49

The Life Other People Want Me to Lead	50
The Uncomprehending Glance	52
Two Men Selling Orchids in a Flower Shop	53
Where to Read Poetry	54
Feeding You Raspberries in the Car	55
Fifth Sitting for a Portrait	56
Making Light of Touch	57
From a High Iron Balcony	58
A Year in the Nail Salon	59
The Before and After Clinic	61
Another Predictable Moonrise Poem	62
Given the Choice	64

IV

THE LABYRINTH BEYOND

The Fish Stall's Dereliction	69
The Blown Egg	70
The Turning Circle	71
Exile	72
Intercepted	73
Ocean Burial	74
Conviction	75
Inference	76

NOTES	79

It must be visible or invisible,
Invisible or visible or both:
A seeing and unseeing in the eye.
> *Wallace Stevens*

Now see the invisible.
> *Rumi*

I
The Edge of Possibility

ASK ICARUS

A contour does not necessarily describe a volume,
or a tourguide a cathedral. In the space
between an object and the point where its shadow
falls, so much can happen; just as the sound
in a musician's head is seldom the same
as the sound his hands draw from the instrument.

Yet we go on expecting a line to encompass
whatever we want of it, as if poetry could be
anything we felt – a metaphysical cartography.
Is the triumph all in the aspiration, the moment
when words lift themselves out of the prosaic
and take wing, or the belief that precludes failure?

TRANSITION

Two clear bags bulging with water,
and two inch-long fish – not gold in fact
but brilliant clementine – flickering
in their airtight, watertight captivity,

each lens distorting like a fairground mirror.
All around the daily mirage seemed to depend
on these two tiny fish, confined but restless,
still in their element though displaced,

every scale steeped in a concentrate
no amount of water could dilute.
Live embers, they upstaged the sunset
while we, commuters on the ferry, passed

from one screen at the office to another
in the living room, shifted from foot to foot
behind the scrim of evening with nothing
but these two brilliant fish making sense.

THE CAPSULE TEST

Having smuggled a small spirit level on board,
I take it from my breast pocket at high altitude
and hold it steady on my knees, its bilious liquor
and airlock – centred, clear as a jewel – dependable
in the glass reservoir. Impartial but absorbed,

I watch as a lost explorer would his compass,
the needle's tremor, but as we swerve and shudder
through the slew of sky its bubble remains true
not to gravity, but the centrifuge. I stare, unmoving
and unmoved, as if my calling were being tested.

VEGETABLE CARVING IN THE NEPTUNE LOUNGE

Was it boredom or curiosity that got us there?
Either way we kept a little irony in reserve,
a twist of self-consciousness. Ridiculous really,
going to watch an aubergine metamorphose
into a dolphin all tricked out with flippers and snout
sculpted from slivers of carrot, transfixed
on a cocktail stick, breasting a cantaloupe wave.

But we clapped Ariel, was it, from Bali,
serene as he was enigmatic. Next,
a hard-boiled egg played havoc with all sense
of scale, conjured into a sperm whale;
then along came a penguin, resolute
on radish feet, and like children free
of sophistication we were utterly charmed

by its innocence, its pith and olive eyes.
Where would contrivance end? In low relief
– a cameo of rind carved to reveal a helmet,
a visor, before the whole lemon was impaled
on a lobster, upstanding, claws tilted to joust.
We sat there in silence, enthralled by artifice,
watching discs of cucumber scallop the flank

of a salamander with watermelon fangs
and parsnip juliennes for antennae,
and if we wondered what *is* the point,
what we asked was all about training,
blades, acidulation. He seemed to exist
less and less as his menagerie assembled
on skewers, peppercorn pupils staring back

from their new-fangled world where peel
coiled and crinkled into a sudden rose
and a translucent lotus was honeydew.
His *pièce de résistance*? A dove, naturally,
neck and feathers pale apple flesh; by now
all sense of the bizarre had given way
to wonderment, pure puppet-theatre

fascination as he, omnipotent, went on
fashioning myths, rearranging the elements
with quiet virtuosity, yoking a seahorse
to a chariot for a mermaid whose cool
and buttery complexion was imperilled
as much by sunlight as the breath we held
while an ice-galleon glittered and dripped into thin air.

TRAVELLING WITH MY THEREMIN

Whenever I'm challenged at check-in
and asked to perform – in jest (Istanbul)
or earnest (Azerbaijan) – I hand out
signed copies of my latest CD. The photo
makes me look presentable as a well-turned
phrase. Customs? They usher me through

all smiles. You don't know exactly
how a theremin works either, do you?
Like a charm . . . Look, it's a pretext.
I don't take risks just for kicks – it's hard
graft being a mule, and what I smuggle
means a great deal further down the line.

DISLOCATION

At the centre of this asymmetrical field
was a gate – free-standing, a thing apart.
Wild fuchsia hedged the field's perimeter;
I remember a tangle of buds like broken veins,

the brackish air, peat that amplified each step
sucking at sodden leather welts, and a residue
of mist that refused to settle into dew, or drift.
A gate without a fence – no evidence

of disassembled stone, no snare of twisted cable,
just two stout posts supporting a hinged frame
pale as driftwood and crusty with lichen.
Did the sullen air rise up and insist

on a password; did the posts themselves
turn into sentries, sentinels; did the gate
swing wide for the wind or close against it?
Was there, in this uncertain light, a gate at all?

DELIRIUM

So much for the young wives' tales – the threat
of darts in the bloodstream lodging in the soft
tissue of the heart; of sirens luring me deeper,
further, sleep-swimming till I'd wake too late
gagging on gelatinous seaweed, lungs bloated

with salty moonlight . . . Jabbed in my hand
the little barbs flared up fierce as blackheads
festering. Iodine, tweezers: useless. But I knew,
needling, it wasn't relief I wanted, but to relive
the stealth and dazzle of Sardinian shallows

where I lost my foothold, and involuntarily
broke my fall with an outstretched hand shocked
by the stiff gristly resistance of an urchin's spines
puncturing. Deep. Immediately what came to mind
was the searing venom of conch and medusa

and the bestiary's mythical porcupine
shooting quills from the quiver of its tail.
Now, having endured that piercing delirium,
I tend the raw cicatrices like a first tattoo
but my palm can still induce that prickly heat,

the sweaty brine, the mirage of a flying fish
launching itself high onto the shingle,
a crazed opal incandescent till the spasms
cease, dulled by the harsh brilliance
that illumines and is irresistible.

COLD-BLOODED SEX

Twenty-five minutes watching a limpet
suck stone while the lagoon's sleek muscle
flexes and withdraws its flagrant glitter.
Sentient, there must be . . . if not moods exactly,
degrees of responsiveness, transitional states
within this cold blind cone that only exists
subject to the green tide's comings and goings.
Thirty-five minutes trying to imagine its life
and I've almost turned it into a verb, but still
it defeats me, effortlessly, and remains
impenetrable. Is its existence pure instinct,
like sex, every reflex purposeful,
every impulse complex only in the analysis?
Can a limpet be fulfilled, or self-absorbed as this?

THE PALACE OF LASSITUDE

Don't think for one moment this is remotely allegorical; I stayed
longer than you'd imagine, stayed till time surrendered its linear
imperatives. I grew a beard deliberating whether to salvage Proust
from the library's silverfish; another watching an albino peahen,
or was it a phoenix, overcome its broodiness. There were mirrors
everywhere, 18th-century Venetian mostly, foxed and oxidising;
whenever one fell it was left where it shattered. Another lost age.
Every so often a truck would drive up, the transfusion service;
enthusiasts among us, pallid as vampires, formed a queue

and sipped, intravenously, through syringes. The rest looked on,
or away, indifferent to anything so obvious as revival, slouched
motionless as the turtles imitating stones in the courtyard pool.
Syrup dispensers hung from the rafters over the terrace – empty
wickless lanterns, their dregs an amber residue; on occasions
dust gathered, violet-grey, and rolled like tumbleweed in slow motion
along the chequered corridors. We watched them accumulate,
    watched
the salon's tapestries fade and disintegrate overnight, the horsehair
    blinds
turned to stencils by a plague of tiny beetles, and the chaise longue

discharging its yellowish stuffing like a whitlow. Irrecoverable.
Impetuous as lichen, a film thickened over iris and cornea, spreading
a haze over everything; it was like looking through a Lalique bowl.
Our only motive was to eke out the delirium between sleep
and daydream, daydream and sleep, exempt from the subtlest forms
of opprobrium and the desultory cycle of appetite, distaste, excretion,
tedium, appetite, distaste . . . Tranquillisers were no more use
than the hallucinogens some of the ex-visionaries still yearned for;
who, after all, would administer them, who procure?

The morning a breeze delivered a humming bird feather to my feet
– nails half rotted with neglect – I knew it was time to leave. By now
exacting as a gnomon and expert in deciphering light's diurnal odyssey
I knew precisely what was meant, the terms intended, what to infer,
and left without a word, without longing or belongings, without a
    glance
at the tin and turquoise effigies, the veranda's rain-polished grain,
the voluptuous vacancy of unlit rooms, and the refectory – irrelevant,
stacked with copper moulds of mythical leopards, dragons, gazelles –
and let time resume its one-sided discourse, its imperious watch.

PATERSON'S CURSE, SALVATION JANE

From this height the salt-flats are oyster shells,
sandblasted mother-of-pearl,
and the only visible road is needle-etched
– abstract geometry.

I squeeze lime juice over chilled papaya.
The Lebanese man at my elbow deletes
and rewrites his Immigration Form.
Point of arrival . . . he asks, *does it mean*
'Visiting relatives'? Or Sydney?

Between in-flight movies and warped sleep
our watch hands swivel through date-lines,
dizzy with keeping up. Where was it, exactly,
the equator split one particle of sea from another?
I try to imagine something palpable
as the meridian at Greenwich, inlaid brass
straddled by photogenic children;
or the language barrier.

* * *

Stacked above the Melbourne runway
wingtips swerve like huge butterknives
spiralling, keeping us all in suspense.

I turn to my phrasebook again.
Repetition makes each syllable inane;
even the magazines' bright flightpath maps
alienate things more by naming them:
Wagga Wagga, Cootamundra, Cupacumbalong.

Will I learn single words to describe
a mineral trace in a parched gully
gravel excavated by honey ants
a cicada's brittle husk
the essential blue of the blue-tongued lizard?

THE MIDNIGHT SCHOLAR

works on little-known poems –
4th- and 5th-century Chinese.

Du Tzu and Fung Xi
are his speciality.

It's extremely unlikely
you'll have heard of them.

He puts his versions on the web
and corresponds with students doing PhDs

in Nairobi
and the Philippines

who ask about the more obscure
classical allusions. Actually

he doesn't speak a word of Cantonese
or Mandarin, but likes making notes

and there's an acupuncturist in Soho
with a window display of grisly

specimens in Petri dishes
shrivelled up and labelled meticulously

Cloud-ear Fungus, Blue Algae,
Powdered Seahorse, Pangolin . . .

THINKING ABOUT PLANTAINS IN THE RAIN

Oblique rain, like a woodblock print
by Hokusai, brings fishing nets to mind,
skein upon skein looped along the shore
of a deserted village; and Du Mu's
cherished weeds, resilient as ever,
each sprung stem juddering, rain-struck.

Let rain, cooler than blood, soothe
my eyelids clenched like a new-born's;
let my lips be startled apart to taste
and overbrim with rain; then may I
enter the condition that precedes
every artist's subtle transpositions,

before the blade is whetted and raised
to incise the grain, or the block is cut
from the trunk, or the axe bites deep
into green sap. Long before that, rain fell
and plantains flourished unlike anything,
without thought entering at all.

SIX MISAPPREHENSIONS
arising from *Quelques Poèmes de Jules Laforgue*, 1973

for Marco Livingstone

Patrick Caulfield produced a series of prints illustrating *Quelques Poèmes de Jules Laforgue*, six of which were included in an exhibition at the Museum of Contemporary Art in Sydney in 2007. The French titles are Laforgue's, the misapprehensions my own.

I
Que ma vie fait envie

COMPLACENCY AND A TWO-WAY MIRROR

Life itself makes me envy my youth
– that protracted dalliance with time
in hand. Now? Now I hold only myself
to blame, only myself in check. Still
after all these years my thumbnail's stained
with the burgundy rind of a mangosteen,
the first I ever peeled, and my tongue
is imprinted with its sweetness – unique,
indelible, unsurpassed. Youth made me
envious of the lives I imagined others lived –
so much more vivid, exotic and risqué.
How many kinds of virginity were there
for me to lose? I rued them all, one by one
... only the stain of a taste endures.

II
Et moi, je suis seul dans ma demeure

IN TIME OF FAMINE

What I craved was to be shameless
somehow, anyhow, to escape my skin
and my limbs' slender transparency and
the naivety I knew others couldn't help
but see right through. It scalds, remember,
to realise your gaucherie's been on parade.
Such blatant inexperience, when the present
sizzles like fat on a hotplate, and when time
aches like a wisdom tooth in the gum . . .
Show me the orchards of knowledge and I
will gnaw the bark right down to the sap
like a famished goat and then spring up
each ring-barked trunk to feast on the bitter
and the ripe indiscriminately, without shame.

III
Je n'ai que l'amitié des chambres d'hôtel

THE PLEASURE OF DECEPTIONS

There's a nuance peculiar to the loneliness
one feels in a hotel room; it's most acute
in Montmartre with a view of rainy slates
and an antique crocheted counterpane.
Here one might almost have merged into
a small Gwen John, except for the greasy
light switch and the absence of an enamel jug.

Even a single bed gives off that frisson
of fresh linen and recent sex. I undress
and masturbate idly thinking of Rodin,
suddenly hungry for samphire, sea salt.
How good the French are at placing mirrors,
seeing their potential, like Cocteau. Displaced,
self-absorbed, loneliness has a scent all its own.

IV
Ah! Nuées accourues des côtes de la Manche

THE OPPOSITE OF A BLAZON

There's something unseemly, even debased
about these streakers' genitals jiggling past –
emasculated rubber grapes, conspicuously
bouncy instead of being ardent, their status
as the most persuasive orators (albeit
speechlessly) on passion's behalf
so compromised, reduced to this elastic
comedy. Who wants virility debunked?
Better a tragedy of manners than this.
So too with breasts. Allow the nipple to be
chaste or a fetish; let it transcend eloquence;
let it jet or console, or let it alone, anything
but this jaunt along the esplanade exhibiting
all flesh as the lowest common denominator.

V

Son mouchoir me flottait sur le Rhin

I KEEP MY LOBSTER ON THE PHONE

I've never really rated the Surrealists.
Too easy by half to juxtapose the bizarre
and the commonplace. Life is one fling
after another anyway, and don't we all learn
how expedient it can be to turn a blind eye
and pass on? As for Dada . . . hardly poetry;
the effect's too short-lived, like a wet dream.
(If you've been counting, expecting a turn
here, you'll be all wrong-footed. Tristan,
darling, *you* come up with a more original
twist.) Besides, this preoccupation with
placement smacks of the *petit bourgeois*.
How to refresh a jejune palate? Let me count
the ways (line 14 and I'm just hitting my stride . . .

VI

Moi je veux vivre monotone

NEVER MISTAKE PASSIVITY FOR BLISS

What does Gymnopédie actually mean
M. Satie? Beside the point. What I yearn for
like a restless convalescent is inertia's lull.
It's nothing to do with lullabies – sleep
is not monotonous, it's a foretaste of death.
Nor is it to do with stasis. There's rhythm
in it. But how to prolong the moment between

a wave's collapse and the sea's regathering,
before the water is dragged and charged
with momentum again. Look at me my love,
this, now, is the best – not before lovemaking
or immediately afterwards, but when the present
extends like a snail's eye into the silence
where everything can be said and thought and felt.

TELLING TALES

Six pairs of knickers strewn along the street
in this sweltering heat, and a story
clinging to each no doubt: the clean,
the none too clean, the raunchy red,
the oyster silk camiknicks (slightly ripped,
since you're a stickler for particulars)
an innocent pair for the firemen's eyes
and last, and least, a tiger-print thong.
I, who have for several years professed
a high-minded indifference to narrative
because of its tiresome sequential diktats
and the charmless way *this* must follow *that*
in quick or, worse, protracted succession,
am intrigued by the *sotto voce* histories
conjured by these cast-offs, these castaways
conspicuously adrift on the sun-smacked Rue Duhesme
right in the heart of *historique* Montmartre.
Fear not, I won't now recount six tawdry episodes,
six essays in abandonment, nor embark
on a discourse concerning *nostalgie de la boue*
and its pervy allure, nor catalogue the ravishing
and impetuous conquests of a hirsute lothario
(shall I go on? No I thought not . . .)
but let us consider, rather, the probability
of this gaudy assortment fetching up here
and shamelessly snagging our eye as we pass by
mid-way through an innocuous day . . .
or the chances of all six being scooped up –
furtively, furiously, flamboyantly etc.

Actually there weren't six, there were four,
but who could resist the clinch of *six* and *nix*,
and you believed me, didn't you, up till now
when you're suddenly suspicious (rightly so)
and narked at having to call the whole pack
into question, knowing that the improbable
has a way of seeming much more plausible
than the dreary old truth of the matter.
So *mon petit chou-fleur, mon petit voyeur,*
mon lecteur, mon semblable, mon amour,
these lines aren't about knickers at all,
though that's how they took up residence
in your imagination, briefly, isn't it? In fact
they're about that insatiable desire for a story.
And curiosity. And the love of the tell-tale.
Or perhaps they're about a bomb disposal expert
with a penchant for . . . no, let's not go into that.
Come, follow me, insouciant as a *flâneur*
with all the time in the world and let's just see
what else we chance across – no no no
not laid out on the *trottoir* and all contrived
like that . . . *here* is what I mean.

II

Valves of Sensation

ABRUPTLY WITHOUT RESERVE

So it is that this evening as the stain of night
filters into every leaf and every space between,
as light deepens and yields to the night, so it is
that an unseen bird sings briefly
and it is not obvious or beautiful or even expressive,
it is not anything other than a cry whose source
lies beyond any anthem or elegy, beyond the nameable;
an utterance from the soul of a bird that has no soul
crying to hasten night or to forestall it forever
as if its single cry foretold the anguish
this night will bring to lovers and the unloved equally,
to those whose lives merge inseparably as all lives must
with the leaves, their sap, green ink, without delineation.

How can one bird sing for so many
without recourse to eloquence or craft,
sing for those who weep with their griefs
in their arms, more deeply and more inwardly
than the swallowed tears that leave only a trace
of salt in the throat; who weep with the breath,
silently in the silence, unheard, with the mute leaves
that are no longer green but have already relinquished
their individual tongues, giving back to the night
everything they borrowed from it,
the density and solemnity it otherwise would lack.

THE IMPLACABLE DETAIL OF MORNING

One more sunrise, another suburban garden:
    why imagine words might somehow substitute
for an everyday vision when the common-
    place passes overlooked – like text, skimmed?
As if, today, the unembellished hand
    could commend to the eye a particular strand
of bindweed spiralling through the camellia,
    and a wren – exuberant, territorial – riddling
the shadows between its evergreen leaves.

Along the terrace each bird's-eye plot
    would be indistinguishable from the next
if it weren't for the details making each
    singular and specific. Unremarkable,
perhaps, but in this act, this observance,
    I want to be vigilant – exacting
in how I now recall you, and precise
    so as to mourn what made unique
your lean, modest, hirsute body,

the mildness of your indignation,
    and your unsettling sensitivity, so acute
I longed to draw out the threat of its dark sting,
    like one of those malignant spiny creatures
exorcised from the mouth in a Romanesque fresco.
    So definitive a portrayal of the afterlife . . .
as if to convince the onlooker in eternity
    even a schematic, perfunctory angel
could be trusted to minister such a blessing.

SLEEPLESS AT DAWN

What comes to mind is the canary
brought up with nightingales
whose improvisations it learned to imitate
and, knowing no other, believed were its own.

ADMISSION AT ALMOND TIME

When I long to draw down blinds against the too insistent world,
even to eclipse the almond tree and its encaustic magnificence,
to close up every sense like a wound, every opening and pore
through which the fierceness of the present impresses itself upon me,
I know, then, that something like grit must settle through the hourglass
in my throat into a deeper reservoir; know how precipitous the spine is,
a tower of pebbles balanced only once on the shore of an inland sea
with the tide lapping, lapping until it collapses back into sand.
Only then can the body's purest distillation be released, let free
as if to search for its source unconditionally, knowing nothing
but the sense of abandonment, and the abandonment of sense.

METEMPSYCHOSIS AND THE PAINTED LADY

He was glad of the sink and liquid soap,
the sound of monsoon rain outside.
Dressing in the dark he said, *Do butterflies*
have any recollection of life before life
(the scent of frangipani would be with him for hours)
or imagine there's only death after death?

Once he'd left, she stood at the window
and watched the rain, watched the rain
sluice over the veins of the frangipani leaves.
Later, retouching her lips, she thought, *Water*
falls and flows, evaporates and falls again;
remember nothing, imagine nothing, be like rain.

THE MERCURY FOUNTAIN

Light-fingered, how long would you
have gone on filching quicksilver,
snapping ampoules from thermometers
and barometers? You even put in a request
for the scraps, the tiny ball bearings, left over
from the dentist's amalgam. Surface tension
made each seed-pearl roll, intent on separation,
and yet they all pooled into one impenetrable
element that flowed – cool but molten, lustrous
as gold, unbeatable, and bright as a witch-ball.

You made it tempting, *Go on, it's like . . .
runny lead under your tongue,* intoxicated,
but I was uneasy, reluctant to hazard
any unfamiliar taste. I only ever asked why
you hoarded it in that big old vacuum flask
where each new globule was assimilated
instantaneously, an emblem of something
elusive as the parts of speech that mystified me.
Who'd have taken you seriously if you'd revealed
the blueprints you kept so carefully hidden?

I was absorbed by my crystal gardens,
jagged encrustations that formed on cotton
dangled in solutions innocuous as glycerine.
At night by torchlight I'd watch the Kilner jars
and aquarium I'd improvised until my eyes
smarted, trying to catch a crystal in the act
of forming. Once when you came to stay
I pocketed a fistful of coffee sugar, a feast
of rough topaz granules to sustain our vigil
across the night, but you gave in to sleep

and by morning were bored by the strings
of sugar quartz and cobalt icebergs that grew
without being alive. But you set about
accumulating the means to make mercury
stream perpetually – and stream it did,
pooling in the palm, spilling between fingers,
splashing into gravel where it shivered
like a demented creature cloning itself
spontaneously before skittering off.
Could you ever have saved enough

to realise your heavy fountainhead?
And if you had, how long would it have played
before being vandalised by someone
tantalised by your design – just as the rabid,
tormented by thirst, are crazed by the sight
of water being poured from a jug –
who'd have kicked the counterbalanced tiers
and stamped the runnels of mercury back
into the earth's deep fissures, maddened
by what they couldn't grasp, or have imagined?

III

Almost Like a Stranger

THE OPACITY OF STRANGENESS

As soon as the April hailstorm ended
my new Somali neighbour
crunched to the middle of his lawn
gathered up a handful of hailstones
and took them back indoors
. . . *to pierce with a hot needle*
and thread on fuse wire like seed pearls.

We only ever meet in passing,
choosing limes in the corner shop,
picking over the star anise, deferential
as students at an evening class
practising idioms, turns of phrase
. . . *hailstones in the ice-cube tray,*
matching pairs like moonstone earrings.

Today, clipping the privet hedge,
I felt his gaze on the nape of my neck,
that subtle sense the hairline has
. . . *how would topiary translate?*
but the moment I turned he dissolved
like sugar into milk, like shadow into dusk.
Whenever he smiles something escapes me.

GIVEAWAY

Hardly one to drop small change
into a busker's grimy fiddlecase
just to assuage the uneasiness
a down-and-out musician induces
in a professional, you stopped
right there on the concourse
and gave him a fiddle lesson instead.

You'd given more than one to me –
conspiratorial with Viennese fingerings,
conversant with those tell-tale bars
in Mendelssohn and Mozart that seem
so innocent on the page but have a way
of turning treacherous on stage;
then, the advice on how to charm –

a faultless recitation of *In My Craft
or Sullen Art,* a set piece sure enough,
but one you'd trump by teasing up
a ratty trouser leg to reveal
what you'd so recently acquired –
socks emblazoned *Mr Perfect.*
You and your strategies . . .

We'd crow like rogues, two Don Juans
comparing last night's ravishing sex
and this morning's raw excess, and I
(brought up so modestly) was proud
you schooled me in the dubious arts
of braggadocio. Now it's up to me
to conjure up the best of you

who gave so much away, priceless things
that couldn't be hoarded anyway:
the unabashed bravura impulse,
audacity born of showmanship,
the knack and know-how you had
with a fiddle under your chin, and
that lost-cause, see-through, giveaway grin.

FIVE KOPECKS TO SPEND AFTER BUSKING

Everything I just earned with my mandolin
would buy me . . . would buy *her*
the last two *Flötestückchen*
speckled with caraway seed
and stale, probably

or that plump Dutch Plait
glazed like a toadstool after rain;
we could sit on a bench any old where
and spend all morning unbraiding it,
picking out currants for the sparrows;
if it were Tuesday I'd have a pocketful of jam
– apricot, in foil sachets Petrovitch pilfers
from Hotel Warsaw for me

or six (and some broken bits) crumbly biscuits,
leftover sweetpaste squeezed through a nozzle
onto oiled paper and dried overnight
in the bread oven – except that thrift
is charmless in a gift

or a slice of plum flan –
caramelised, impossible to divide
and knowing her she'd refuse . . .

or a great wedge of sourdough
no no no

or one just *one*
croissant
grinning gold from ear to ear
if only there were one

THE LIFE OTHER PEOPLE WANT ME TO LEAD

is quite unlike my own;
they hold me up in their imaginations like a vanilla pod,
improbable and slightly exotic but familiar as Muscovado sugar;
they want me to read obsessively – books more abstract
than any they can be bothered with – and have a lot of sex,
sufficiently complicated sex that they can think about it hard
while knowing it's probably not for them;
they want me to wear expensive old shirts and expensive new
    underwear
and make Greek coffee with cardamom and squeeze fresh
    tangerines first thing
and they want to hear my crotchety green parakeet from Madras
    mutter

Come up and see my etchings sometime

and they expect me to navigate the Tokyo Fish Market at 5 a.m.
and the Covered Bazaar in Istanbul at the drop of a hat
and know where to buy *marrons glacés* in June;
they want me to have a Cézanne watercolour of bread and melons
    in the yellow bedroom
and kindling laid in every grate ready to blaze when kissed by a
    single spill
and a huge basket of fir cones from Provence to hand
and a spillage of butter-stained love poems on the kitchen table
and an inexhaustible supply of pistachios and macadamia nuts;
they want me to drink *Beaumes de Venise* in a brocade smoking jacket
and clip my topiary hedge by hand and know the libretto of *Figaro*
as well as lyrics sung by Piaf, Jacques Brel and Gardel;
they want me to invite them to my *palazzo* on the Grand Canal
to sip Prosecco on a balcony swagged with magenta petunias

and discuss the cost of hiring a gondola for the night, and a gigolo;
they want to hear my African Grey imitate their mobile phone

weep weep, weep weep

while I rustle up risotto with fresh porcini in no time
and console them for having landed up with the wrong husband
    again;
they want introductions to fado, tango, neo-classical Stravinsky
and my favourite, my most exquisite Rose-cheeked Macaw
that screams at the most inappropriate moment

J'arrive, j'arrive

and they want to fossick around in my bedside cabinet and find
    it's full of Keats
and treats and Japanese dildos made of horn such as they've never
    seen before;
they want the hours to pass more slowly through all my beautiful
    clocks
and they want me never to get the slightest bit bored, least of all
    with them;
they want my Sulphur-crested Cockatoo to recite on demand
the complete works of Blake starting with

O rose thou art sick

and expect me to have a cache of fireflies in the freezer that I alone
can breathe into life and make flicker just for tonight . . . and
    I do, I do.

THE UNCOMPREHENDING GLANCE

Mid-day, the ornamental pear tree's silhouette
is razored, but the focal point is diamond cut
– a glass bowl in a woman's lap with cantaloupe
and honeydew glazed like chunks of cornelian
and onyx. Three red-eyed choughs stalk about

on the touchpaper lawn, distinct in the distance,
their claws definitive as the shadows that retract,
sharp enough for shadow puppets. She gazes up
into the shimmering canopy of leaves, reflective,
as if they might retrieve an elusive turn of phrase

or encrypt some subtlety in her expression.
Is it only the light that makes her appear
to define the scene, props disposed knowingly
as a Renaissance saint's inkhorn, or salver
of eyes, emblems to prompt interpretation?

Or could it be less significant than that –
simply a tree eclipsing some vague disaffection
or anxiety the way a Green Room soothes
a frazzled actor? And what of the inclination
to attribute motive, to layer and overlay

a face like this glimpsed in a moment of stasis,
unselfconscious under translucent leaves,
when it may be irreducible, may mean nothing
more than a frame left unexposed on a spool,
blank among the conscientious poses?

TWO MEN SELLING ORCHIDS IN A FLOWER SHOP

You want me to describe them don't you?
The orchids, that is, not the men. Well
I adore lush adjectives too, but my favourite,
orchidaceous, is best used metaphorically
and would be squandered on a phalaenopsis
in Holland Park. Anyway this isn't about looking.
It's about that sudden melancholia
flowershops induce in me: those deathly buckets
and the mingled smell of too many flowers,
expensive things you can live without,
and underlying everything the protracted last
gasp of perishable vegetation. What would I do
with a truss of blooms flown in from Singapore
so lurid and so succulent they look carnivorous?

Of course I'm tempted to enter
their ferny, moist interior and lift
something improbable – six gerberas
and a varnished gourd would do – if only
to see what sort of outcry would ensue.
Would they come for me, wreathed
in window-dressings (Chinese gooseberries
and firecracker chillies strung on red twine)
grimacing like a reception committee
on the runway at Honolulu? Between them
they're keeping more than an eye on me, sidelong
can tell at a glance my bathroom wouldn't suit,
that my habits and décor are all wrong for them.
The flowers, I mean, not the men.

WHERE TO READ POETRY

Larkin on the Shinkansen
Hopkins in a Ford Fiesta
Dickinson in an opium den
Whitman in a Sushi Bar
e. e. cummings and Jeremy Prynne
at your wit's end, and only then
Wordsworth to a concubine
Basho on the Circle Line.

FEEDING YOU RASPBERRIES IN THE CAR

This is not prescribed in the Kama Sutra
but one by one I choose the most succulent
and present them to your lips.

I know you love raspberries. I know you love me.
But if I ask myself *In what does love consist? –
in which instant can love be known
and known to be expressed?*
the answer is simply This.

Paradise is at my fingertips,
in this punnet, in your mouth.
Nowhere else in the whole galaxy
could I find for you eight berries
more perfect than these which are to hand.

Outside, torrential midsummer rain
flings itself at the windscreen
as if imploring that we let it in, declaiming
that water swelled each capsule,
that water is all one element
however divided it might be, provisionally,
and that water is the image
I had not known I was looking for –
an image of love, of the flux of love,
constant, yet constantly changing.

But what need have we of imagery now?
We have seven raspberries,
we have the moment,
sunlight, rain and one another.
Love, this is all, and this is enough.

FIFTH SITTING FOR A PORTRAIT

Glass is not disinterested, just cool;
knowing both molten and crystalline states
it asks, *Why should transparency be seen
as impartial? As anything?*

North lit, your Talgarth Road studio
is a homage to the glazier's craft, but each pane
crops whatever it reveals, like every definition.
Bored by aphorisms and this pose, stupefied

by now, I ask myself what I'd do if I could move.
Soften like wax and undress you – saffron cheesecloth
– absorbed, distracted by a strand of hair . . . revelation
does not come simply for having been sought

nor will it slope away quietly should paint catch light.
That's why, like a tongue seeking out a tender tooth,
I go on sitting for you at this window, aching for
the sudden access of crocus, sparrow hawk, snow.

MAKING LIGHT OF TOUCH

One ride in a time machine?
I'd choose the game of billiards
when touch, grace, poise, finesse
got the better of brute force
and Napoleon lost to Josephine.

It's not that I want to disparage
power; the will can overrule
frost-bitten flesh and make a hero
out of a milksop. Some things
can only be achieved through grit

and bloody-mindedness; others
thrive on being forced, like rhubarb.
But I've learnt how senseless it is
to try to coerce a cello into
making a more beautiful sound.

However resolute, there's a limit
to what a muscle can grasp; caprice
may make the tennis racket sing
unpredictably, and when we hear
the sweet spot ring we know

determination can't entirely claim
or explain this felicity. The Muse
won't knuckle down and comply
because an artist's put the hours in;
no, diligence won't do the trick. But

when Josephine put down her cue
did she laugh it off, or smile a little
mystified by this mischievous gift –
deftness that appeared effortless,
oblivious (almost) to victory?

FROM A HIGH IRON BALCONY

If I brought you back a salamander,
six terracotta bowls for gazpacho,
a slab of pistachio nougat or salt cod
from the fly-blown market,
would you be touched? Or amused?

From here I sense in you a new simplicity,
the contemplative's austerity; besides,
you already have more kelims than floor space,
Georgian candlesticks but not the moment,
or the guest, to find them indispensable.

At present you're absorbed
by the flame in the iris. So here, instead,
is something insubstantial – a luminous view.
It begins with a chipped crock on a windowsill,
a still life by Zurbarán of quinces and shallots,

and it leads through acid-bitten glass
into a courtyard rusty with fountains
where six parakeets are feasting
high in the palms on clusters of amber dates . . .
and it ends in a lattice of wrought iron

tendrils and fronds of seaweed
casting a stencil of shadow across
a rickety wicker table where a man
in linen is twisting his propelling pencil
on the brink of writing you this.

A YEAR IN THE NAIL SALON

I

The first day of spring takes everyone by surprise:
one morning, unannounced, the light will clarify
pale gold, as if rinsed in dilute honey, and suddenly
windows all along the terrace will need cleaning.
In the Nail Salon the new range gleams, *Sea Fern,
First Blush, Tourmaline;* in the sodden flowerbeds
clumps of crocuses flare like new-born galaxies
30 million light-years away. Purposeful suburban birds
busy themselves, garnering shreds of garden twine
and raffia to dangle, triumphant, from their beaks.
Skin feels air-brushed, air-kissed, freshly susceptible
to the tentative touch, to all the pleasures of exposure.
Young couples sit on their doorsteps sipping coffee
under an eggshell heaven, and everything seems possible.

II

Summer's one cliché after another, and everybody loves it,
even the girls who dither and wince, waxing their bikini lines.
In Brick Lane the espadrilles appear again – fuchsia, turquoise,
and at the Nail Salon the bottles gleam like cabochons
impatient to glaze those pasty stubs *Frosted Mulberry,
Rouge Noir, Pompeii Purple*. Summer makes things easy
with one long exhalation of desire, one long Bombay Sapphire
after another, with the simple thirst for cider, cordials,
jugs of home-made lemonade clanking with ice cubes
the kids will fish out one by one and suck into oblivion.
Then there's Summer Pudding, dark as clotted blood
with a dollop of clotted cream, and everywhere a lassitude
and slackness in the eyes as desire dissolves into night, knowing
that seduction will be exquisite, and effortless as tickling trout.

III

Nostrils flinch in the astringent air, and underpaid shopgirls
in nippy nylon console themselves by folding and refolding
the stacks of cashmere stoles. The Nail Salon smoulders:
Silk Route Cinnabar, Burnt Caramel, Agent Provocateur.
By day, the conference pears rot as they ripen, hollowed out
by a phalanx of intoxicated wasps, the sky is an ocean swirled
by shoals of starlings, and squirrels squirrel away their spoils,
greed masquerading as prudence. The kitchen window weeps
with the sweetness of parsnips roasting; on the windowsill
six waxy conkers gleam like burnished trophy. The crab-apple
tautens under its burden, each branch flexing with the slow
deliberation of an archer aiming for the stars. By night,
the moon swells low over the allotments, a gilded pumpkin
just out of reach, and tantalising – the patron saint of scrumping.

IV

When else would anyone feign delight over a pair
of satin boxer shorts emblazoned with horny reindeer?
When else do chips stinging with salt and malt vinegar
taste so good that the sleet and cancelled bus are forgettable?
The Nail Salon's neglected lacquers sulk and separate:
Cloisonné, Java Jade, Ingénue, Tahitian Pearl.
Winter isn't crystalline, or pristine – just gritty pavements,
laundry mouldering over the bath, and a smelly labrador
steaming by the radiator. Nothing kills romance so fast
as a morning-after hotwater bottle congealed in the sheets.
But the provident lover has mulled wine and baked apples,
has a cache of dried tangerine rind to throw on the fire.
It's midnight, he whispers, and the flames turn green
as he inches his fingers towards the crucible of desire.

THE BEFORE AND AFTER CLINIC

All over Manchester balding scalps
which were till recently a problem
are passing undetected, rugged
and luxuriously mussed. Now

and now is ever after you'd never guess.
Clump by surreptitious clump
the little transplants thrive,
striking, just like brambles.

Two photos side by side
show there's nothing to betray
the stages in-between that tonsure
unsightly and this hirsute shock,

but where did all the grafted tussocks
come from? Somewhere there must be
a symmetry of tell-tale missing bits,
equally unseen, perfectly healed

presumably, the invisible
mender's handiwork *are you
so easily persuaded?* overlooked
in the throng of follicles.

ANOTHER PREDICTABLE MOONRISE POEM

Sulphurous as tiger's eye (who's used that before?) or adamantine
(what *is* adamantine? – oh those nouns that trick you into thinking
they're adjectives or vice versa) and fat as an engorged . . . no, not fat
as anything, just huge and yellow – except that four measly syllables
won't suffice to make a poem of it, not even for a frugal Zen recluse
in his snowy mountain hermitage watching the same moon rise –
and I feel moved, like so many, and what's more
would like you to feel moved too – an innocent enough motive
if not entirely divorced from the carnal – but who can hazard
anything insightful about the ethics of the poetic impulse? So . . .
to begin again, an enormous sherbet lemon of a moonrise
behind the dome of Santa Maria della Salute (see any cheap guide
    to Venice)
couldn't be more of a cliché, reducing the entire night to a postcard
and making everyone want to lunge for their lover's lips to put it
    politely.
Instant romance, just add fluid. But I ask you: what is one to do
with this recurrent impulse prompted by the recurrent moon,
this convention that can still whack me in the solar plexus
and halt my most predictable feet? My own sad steps. And how
can the desire to find words . . . no, how can the same old words
    aspire
to live up to the desire, in the absence of astounding originality?
    Quite so.
But the moon is not at all original and nor am I. Why strive like this?
Should I, rather, describe the *thwump* in the diaphragm just as I feel it
instead of outlining the moon as it intersects with Longhena's cupola;
or fast forward and go into the fantasy of your passionate mouth,
the squid-ink night, the lap-dancing lagoon and the inevitable
    orgasm?
Isn't that almost as obvious as the phases of the moon itself?
O sexual moon; O Japanese-rabbit-staring-at-the-moon; O moon-faced lunacy

Remember how Ted Hughes stressed the word 'God*dess*' and all you
    could think was
how 1940s-screen-idol it sounded, not like poetry at all?
But then what *is* like poetry? What's poetry *like*? None the wiser,
the moon goes on mounting Santa Maria, not rapacious but
    unstoppable.
Which reminds me: did you ever as a child open your fist deliberately
to release a helium balloon and relish the euphoria of no more tugging,
of giving desire away, giving way to desire; the consummation
of the sky's complete receptivity, and the unhindered nothingness
between a muscly clump of fingers and infinity? Yes. But can you
    recall
the exact moment when you *stopped* thinking about that gaseous
    bubble
so distant and so diminished it was hardly more than a floater in
    your eye?
That moment of forgetting, *that* is what this moon appears to insist
    on now,
as if to present to my complacent retina an image so vivid, so
    imperious,
a vision so conspicuous it could coalesce all the neglected, familiar
overlooked and overworked clichés of moon into one, and command
    immediacy.
Of course I can't stay with it long; can't endure to see a thing
as revelation for long – but at least let the impulse endure
for as long as it takes to write this. And then? Or, more precisely, now
let's return to our unoriginal bed and be unoriginal lovers all over
    again,
but as if for the first and the very last time at once. But before we do,
can I just ask what you feel about *r*omance as opposed to rom*a*nce?

GIVEN THE CHOICE

you'd rather be the moon's reflection
than the moon itself, you say.
Reflection you say, but it exists
everywhere simultaneously

while the moon goes on being
singular and self-absorbed as me.
Should this be construed as indicative
– to do with gender; a sad reflection?

Isn't the moon almost always she?
So I'll ask again, not of either of us
but into the night, and let myself be
all the waters of the world,

ocean, puddle, inland sea,
there to receive you like a touch
of silver on a tear that leaves
you undiminished, but gilds me.

IV

The Labyrinth Beyond

THE FISH STALL'S DERELICTION

Was there a shivering in the air or light, as if on the periphery
of vision something vital flickered and suddenly condensed,
sufficient to conjure a subtle sense, almost a sensory mirage
of what had gone overlooked? Not shimmering – less glamorous
than that, and more elusive – but a feeling that these flagstones
where crates of crushed ice spilled and vaporised still retained

a trace of thawing squid, an after-image of mackerel opalescent
in polystyrene trays, scallop-shell middens, shrimps translucent
and brittle as articulated glass, and all the incalculable brilliance
of salt water and sweet, just as when the wasps gathered, zinging,
hungry for pungent blood and the severed fins lobbed into buckets
of offcuts and the jelly eyes with their individual drops of ocean.

None of the market's regulars trudging past seemed concerned
by what was no longer there. No one glanced at me, hesitating
next to nothing. Why should they? Everything passes anyway,
dissolving in the welter of being reshaped, replaced; the flux
of being provisional. But the fishstall's vacancy altered every
thing, altered me, no longer queuing, impatient, but transfixed

by the vision laid out, each death transfigured into a still-life
made and remade afresh each day for customers and passers by,
eels and whelks and razor-shells no less representative, their juices
and lives seeping away, the blue crabs bubbling into an endless
sluice of hose and meltwater, the crusty lobsters hunkering down
on ice, manacled in rubber bands, defying death by sunlight.

THE BLOWN EGG

I have kept it till now,
the blown egg – owl, is it,
or simply a pure white hen's?
All he said was

*I have rolled a piece of paper
into this blown egg;
you'll have to break it
to read what it says*

as he placed it gently
in the palm of my hand.
By then his hands were pale
as eggshell, almost as frail.

I have kept it till now,
but now that I know what he meant
there's no need to safeguard
or break into what went unsaid.

THE TURNING CIRCLE

We have not yet driven past a field of sunflowers
but when we do let's stop the car and stand
in the sudden quiet on the verge of nowhere
in particular and look into the close-packed gold.

A plant can no more account for turning
towards the light than I can reassure you.
But we know that nothing exists in isolation,
and so no single flowerhead can claim for itself

some special distinction simply for tracking
the sun's ascendance and decline;
nor is it diminished by being passed over
by the sun's eye, never once singled out.

The sun itself is just one focal point
in a field of far-flung stars – stars which we
find our faces drawn by as the planet turns,
whether the pillow from which we reflect

on the vast incalculable dark is goosedown,
a lover's breast, or the inevitable earth.

EXILE

Perhaps when the conservatory is ready
you'll come to Greenford and we'll talk more...
he smiles, and I imagine the smell of cinnamon
and mace, a dish of persimmons, tiny gilt glasses
on a metal tray and rugs that make me dizzy,
as though the Iraqi light were knotted into the pile
and lying in wait within each cochineal cartouche,
each intricate hallucinogen; my eyes are easy prey

... and if it's not exasperating of me to ask
might you bring your violin and play? I contrive
a patchwork notion of what he's forfeited –
midnight recitations among friends on a rooftop;
citrus fruits blood-warm on the tree, in the palm.
All I can do is imagine these things in miniature
from miniatures flattened of all depth, registered
in the single point perspective of my curiosity.

He'll overlook my ignorance, and with the grace
and composure of someone who's lived through
suffering I know nothing of, ask if I'd agree
baroque ornamentation could be thought to verge
on what is called 'the Arabesque'? Maybe later
we'll discuss the Stalag officer remembered now
for giving manuscript paper to a detainee; and
how much turns on such small acts of generosity.

INTERCEPTED

It's a pomegranate
– stiff as salt fish now
but you can still see here
the hole that went right through.

You have a war museum . . .
I've heard about the cigarette case
dented in a pocket. Is it true?
Here there's a limit

to resistance. This year
the pomegranates are cheap . . .
lovers swap them you know
because the pips stay sweet

long after the skin
has hardened.

OCEAN BURIAL

He stood waist deep in the tepid sea,
and the waves came and came
pushing him back towards the shore.
Impassive, it seemed, with the passivity
that comes of exhausted grief, he remained,
arms exhausted by their burden – the hessian
heavier with each wave, and darkening.

More than any gesture of submission
or surrender, the inclination of his head
was the embodiment of despair
and the renunciation of despair;
beneath his eyebrows the crescents of bone
were abstract, beyond abstraction.
When his arms let float their burden,
let sink their burden
into the indifferent waves, he remained
human past all endurance,
unmoving, ageless, present, enduring
all that remained for him to renounce.

Waist deep in the serpentine sea,
only the ocean pushed him back
towards the sand where each wave broke
and as it broke gave up, gave back
its individuality, ceasing
at the extremity, the line
from which the ebbing tide
would in time withdraw.

CONVICTION

Incapable of cruelty or indulgence, time
shows no interest in its own advancement,
but there are times when such impartiality
seems pitiless. One fallible inmate, convicted
by another fallible body of men, scarcely heard
the judge's sentence – uncommuted, unrevoked.
But before the last indignity of all, the senseless
spasm, what did he pick for his final meal?

Hamburger chilli sauce strawberry ice cream

as if to convince himself even here, even now
within this labyrinth of cells, that a taste
for strawberry could be satisfied unconditionally
just as a migrant bird picks off midges on the wing
oblivious to the shadowless speck suspended
high overhead with the capacity to drop
soundlessly through air, through time, undetected,
out of nowhere – out of the sun's indivisible flame.

INFERENCE

Here is a wall.
There was not a wall here before,
but now there is – irrefutable as a theorem.
There was not a theorem here before,
but now that there is, it has the obdurate
solidity of something laid down in the mind.

What was there before this wall?
What was here before this wall?
Not the prospect of a wall
or the absence of a wall
or even a trace of a neglected wall.

There was an olive grove – leaves,
thousands of tiny fish in an ocean of air,
a shoal of silver, a mirage that shimmered
or was still.

Now there is this and that, depending
on the line you take.
Something has been enforced, reinforced,
and it changes the way thought works.

Or rather, it forces thought to work
in its way only, its only way, defining
what had never felt the want of definition
any more than the edge of the wind
had sought to be pinned down.

I saw the olive trees broken
to make this wall; heard their roots
like bones under concrete,
their fibres torn like nerves.
Then I went numb.

The light here is changed now;
shadow falls where it never fell before.
I watch this wall – it gives nothing away;
I confront it – it yields nothing.
Lizards sun themselves elsewhere.

Fear built this wall
but fear will not surmount it.
Fear is not subject to a line of thought
or any theorem.
Fear is a cast of mind.
And a wall is a cast of mind.

NOTES

The three lines by Wallace Stevens are from *Notes Toward a Supreme Fiction: It Must Be Abstract, VI* in his *Selected Poems* (Faber and Faber, 1953).

The sentence by Jalaluddin Rumi (1207–73) is from the *Mathnawi* (VI, 3487–3510) translated by Coleman Barks in *We Are Three* (Maypop Books, 1987).

All four section headings are Francis Bacon's own words extracted from sentences in *Interviews with Francis Bacon* by David Sylvester (Thames and Hudson, 1975).

* * *

'Ask Icarus'. The first line is from *Bridget Riley, Dialogues on Art* (Zwemmer and Philip Wilson Limited, 1995).

Paterson's Curse, Salvation Jane: two names given to *Echium vulgare*, the blue-flowered plant known in England as Viper's Bugloss, which was introduced to Australia and spread like a weed, saving the sheep from famine but damaging their wool with its burs.

'Thinking About Plantains in the Rain'. The Chinese poet Du Mu (AD 803–852) planted plantains outside his window for the way they moved in the rain. I am indebted to *Plantains in the Rain: selected Chinese poems by Du Mu* translated by R. F. Burton (Wellsweep Press, 1990) for this.

'Giveaway' i.m. Roy Gillard. The bars referred to are: Mendelssohn *Violin Concerto* Op. 64, 1st movement bars 113–120, and Mozart *Violin Concerto in G*, K.261, 1st movement bars 60–61.

'Exile' was written for Fawzi Karim. In 1940 Olivier Messiaen wrote his *Quatuor pour la fin du temps* while detained in Stalag Camp 8A near Görlitz. A German officer gave him manuscript paper and a pen. The first performance was on 15 January 1941, in one of the prison camp's wash-rooms.

'Ocean Burial' was written after watching William Kentridge's film of animated charcoal drawings, *Tide Table*, in the Art Gallery of New South Wales, Sydney, Australia.